A Song
for the
Birds

How Do U MUSIC™

BOOK ONE: A Song for the Birds

©2014 by Leah Wells

Illustrations ©2014 by Naomi Rosenblatt
Cover and book design by Naomi Rosenblatt

HelioTot is an imprint of Heliotrope Books.

A Song
for the Birds

Leah Wells

Illustrated by Naomi Rosenblatt

HelioTot

New York City

For our
wonderful parents

Aaron Rosenblatt and Judy Rosenblatt

The sun is rising on the bay.

The Albatross wakes up and sings her A

The Bluebird sings his **B**

The Canary sings her C

The Duck sings her D

The Eagle sings his E

The Finch sings her F

And the Grackle sings his G...

But the Birdwatcher says:
"A, B, C, D, E, F, G ...
I don't want just one note.
I want to hear a song."

"Why don't you birds sing a song?"

The birds look at
each other
with confusion.

"What's a song?" asks the Grackle.

"I think it
means that we all
sing together,"
says the Finch.

"All right," says the Albatross. "All of us sing A."

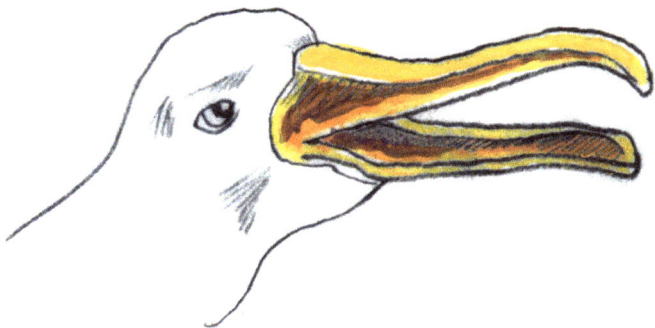

"Better with B!"
cries the Bluebird.

"Can't we sing C?" asks the Canary.

"Do sing D," says the Duck.

"Enough," says the Eagle. "Everyone sing E."

"For me it's F," says the Finch.

"Go with G,"
says the Grackle.

"No. no no. You still don't understand," grumbles the Birdwatcher. "A song has a melody. You sing many notes – one note after another."

The Albatross looks back at
the Bluebird and the Bluebird
looks down at the Duck.
What does he mean?

"Wait. I hear something," says the Canary.
"What's that?" asks the Eagle.

On a branch sits
the Mockingbird.
"Tweedley Dee,
Tweedley Dee!"

He sings two notes, and then three notes together. And then four, and more.

Listen to the Mockingbird

It sounds so pretty.
The other birds
stop arguing to listen.
Now they know what
the Birdwatcher wanted:
a song, like the Mockingbird sings.

But the sun has set.
It is getting late
and the Birdwatcher
went home to sleep
without hearing
a song.

"I think he lives in that red house by the bay," says the Eagle. So all the birds fly down to a tree by his window.

The moon is rising, and stars shine in the sky.

And the birds
know exactly
what to sing.

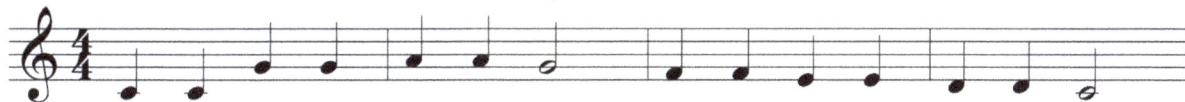

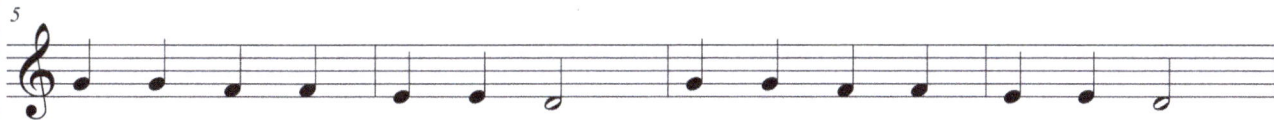

"Twinkle, Twinkle Little Star,
How I wonder what you are!"

About the Author and Illustrator

They're sisters! They live in New York City.

Leah Wells, the younger one, plays stringed instruments – the guitar, banjo, mandolin, and fiddle – and teaches music. She is developing the *How Do You Do Music*™ series to help children read and enjoy music. Her first book, *Games That Sing*, was published in 2011 by Heritage Music Press. Leah is married with two sons.

Naomi Rosenblatt, seated behind on the rocking horse, is a painter, illustrator, designer, and the founder of Heliotrope Books. Together with her sister she is starting the HelioTot imprint for children.

www.ingramcontent.com/pod-product-compliance
Lightning Source LLC
Chambersburg PA
CBHW041633040426
42447CB00019B/3481